Adventure SPORTS

SKIING and Snowboarding

Stephanie Turnbull

A+

Smart Apple Media

Published by Smart Apple Media, an imprint of Black Rabbit Books
P.O. Box 3263, Mankato, Minnesota, 56002
www.blackrabbitbooks.com

Printed in the United States of America, at Corporate Graphics
in North Mankato, Minnesota.

Designed and illustrated by Guy Callaby
Edited by Mary-Jane Wilkins

Cataloging-in-Publication Data is available from
the Library of Congress

ISBN 978-1-62588-387-2

Photo acknowledgements
t = top, b = bottom, l = left, r = right, c = center
page 1 Rafa Irusta; 2t Maxim Blinkov, b J. Helgason; 3 BMJ;
4 Monkey Business Images; 5 IM_photo; 6t Leah-Anne Thompson,
b Vicente Barcelo Varona; 7tr Roberto Caucino, tl dean bertoncelj;
8 Mitch Gunn; 9 Maridav; 10t steve estvanik, b Photick; 11t Fedor
Selivanov, c Photobac; 12t Sergey Nivens, b Andrei Ivashkevich;
13t fluke samed, b Tiplyashina Evgeniya; 14 Tatiana Popova;
15 haveseen; 16 Magnus Kallstrom; 17t Georgina198, b l i g h t
p o e t; 18 Galyna Andrushko; 19l Ihor Pasternak, r Jan Pala;
20 Mitch Gunn; 21l PhotoStock10, r Iurii Osadchi; 22 Evikka;
23l Becky Wass, r Pavel L Photo and Video/
all Shutterstock
Cover Sergey Nivens/Shutterstock

DAD0063
022015
9 8 7 6 5 4 3 2 1

CONTENTS

FEEL THE THRILL

Think you have the skill, strength, and stamina to try skiing or snowboarding? If you like the idea of whizzing down steep slopes at heart-stopping speed, then read on...

Skiing down mountain slopes in dazzling sun is a fantastic experience.

Take the challenge

Imagine the excitement of gliding over hard-packed ice, skidding through powdery snow, or twisting and turning down hills. How about shooting off the end of a ramp and launching into the air? Snowboarding and skiing are seriously extreme sports!

THRILL SEEKER

Simone Origone (Italy)

FEAT
World record for speed skiing:
156.8 mph (252.4 km/h)

WHERE AND WHEN
Les Arcs, France, 2

4

Snowboarding was invented by surfers who adapted their boards to skim over snow instead of waves!

EXTREME BUT TRUE One of the wo... the toughe... runs is La Chavanette, or The Swiss Wall, in France. It's only 0.6 miles (1 km) long, but drop... a dizzying 1,086 feet (... m). Not surprisingly, it's ... erts only.

Tough stuff

Racing over snow on skis or a board is tough. You need good gear, great training, and excellent balance. You must be physically fit, have nerves of steel, and be able to keep calm in tricky situations. And you shouldn't mind falling over!

CLOTHES AND KIT

Dressing sensibly and buying or renting the right gear is essential if you want to enjoy skiing or snowboarding— and not end up cold or injured!

Layer up

The temperature is below freezing in the mountains, but exercise will make you hot, so dress in several thin layers. Start with thermals and finish with a fleece jacket and a windproof or padded jacket and warm pants. Wear gloves, a hat, and goggles to protect your eyes from snow and sun.

Select skis

Skis have a smooth, flat base to slide easily, and a turned-up front so they don't catch in snow.

Sharp, metallic edges bite into the snow when you turn. The longer your skis, the faster you'll go, but don't choose ones taller than you are.

Big boots

Skiing and boarding boots are high and rigid to protect your ankles as you turn. Make sure they fit well and don't rub. Ski boots are designed to clip firmly onto skis but detach easily if you fall.

Ski boot

Snowboarding boot

Choose a board

There are three main types of snowboard. They all have straps to attach to boots.

Freestyle board: Wide, light, short, and flexible. Moves and turns easily. Great for beginners.

Freeride board: A stiffer design, more stable at high speeds. The most popular board.

Alpine board: Long, narrow, and stiff. Best for fast, experienced boarders.

EXTREME BUT TRUE Every year, thousands of people injure themselves skiing or snowboarding —but you could halve your chance of a serious head injury by wearing a helmet.

GET FIT

Skiing and snowboarding are fast, furious sports. The fitter you are, the more fun you'll have on the slopes.

Muscle power

Strong thigh muscles are essential to stay in control as you speed downhill. Good muscle strength will also give you the stamina to power along on flatter ground. Try some of these exercises to tone your thighs.

Two-leg squat

One-leg squat

Split squat **lunge**

1. *Stand with legs shoulder-width apart, arms out in front, knees bent and back straight. Hold the position, then stand up. Repeat a few times.*

2. *Balance on one leg with the other out in front. Slowly bend your knee. See how low you can go, then come up. Just do a few at first—they're hard!*

3. *Stand up and lunge one leg forward. Lower your back knee as far as possible. Hold for five seconds, then come up. Repeat a few times.*

Stre-e-etch!

Don't forget to stretch well after exercise, as it stops your muscles from stiffening up. Here are a few useful stretches.

Groin stretch

Standing **hamstring** stretch

Hip stretch

Standing thigh stretch

EXTREME BUT TRUE Your body responds to exercise by sending extra blood to the muscles you're using, helping them to grow and work better.

START TO SKI

Sliding over snow can be tricky, so make sure you learn how to do it properly. Sign up for classes at ski resorts or visit an **artificial ski slope** nearer home.

Ski resorts run classes led by trained experts. It's a great way to get started and build confidence.

Funny feet

First, get used to wearing skis on flat ground. Try turning in a circle, shifting your weight from one ski to another, and balancing on one ski with the other in the air. It's harder than it looks!

You may feel wobbly at first, but you'll soon get used to balancing on skis.

Slow and steady

Start on a gentle **bunny hill**. Try to keep your skis **parallel** as you slide, then slow down by pushing out with your heels so the tips of the skis move together and the tail ends move out. This is called a snowplow. Press more on one side than the other to turn.

Knowing how to snowplow means you can control your speed effectively.

You can expect to fall over a lot when you're learning to ski!

EXTREME BUT TRUE The higher you go, the less **oxygen** there is, which can leave you gasping for breath if you attempt advanced runs without letting your body adjust first.

THRILL SEEKER

Barbara Hillary (U.S.)

FEAT
First African-American woman to ski to both Poles

WHERE AND WHEN
North Pole 2007
South Pole 2011

BOARDING BASICS

Do you want to experience the thrills and spills of snowboarding? It's tough to learn, but fantastic fun once you can twist, turn, and do tricks.

EXTREME BUT TRUE

Snowboarding stunt experts perform amazing jumps, flips, and spins down slopes, off ramps, and even backward along walls or rails.

Perfect position

Stand sideways to the slope when on your board. Spread your weight evenly on both feet, keep your body and shoulders parallel to the board, and turn your head to look forward over your shoulder.

THRILL SEEKER

Darren Powell (U.S.)

FEAT
World speed snowboarding record: 129.9 mph (201.9 km/h)

WHERE AND WHEN
France, 1999

Move and turn

As you start to move, stay relaxed and flexible, with your knees bent and hands out. Shift your weight forward and lean on your toes or heels, depending on which way you want to turn. If you overbalance, try to land on your knees.

HIT THE SLOPES

Once you've mastered the basics, test your skills on a full ski run. There are fantastic ski resorts and slopes all over the world, many with breathtaking mountain scenery.

Where to go

Skiing isn't cheap, so plan your holiday carefully. Look for resorts that have lots of runs to suit you and find the best time of year to go.

Chair lifts take you to the top of the mountain, where you can choose your run.

THRILL SEEKER

Davo Karnicar (Slovenia)

FEAT
Skied from Mount Everest summit to base camp: 2.48 miles (4 km); vertical drop 11,483 feet (3,500m)

WHERE AND WHEN
Nepal, 2000

Resort runs

Ski resorts mark runs clearly and provide maps of the routes. Machines called **snowcats** keep the snow smooth and flat, and barriers block dangerous areas. Hazards such as trees and fences may be covered in padding to avoid accidents.

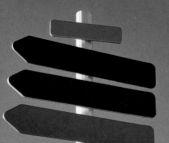

Runs are divided into four grades:

Green: Gentle, easy slopes.

Blue: Steeper and longer, but still good for beginners.

Red: May have narrow or steep sections that need more skill.

Black: Very steep, difficult runs, for experts only.

INTO THE WILD

Want to get away from the crowds for a real outdoor adventure? Pack a map, compass, and emergency supplies and head into the wild!

Back-country action

Once you're an expert skier or boarder, try **back-country** slopes. These aren't smooth, so they're much more challenging. But beware— you risk getting lost or even caught in an avalanche.

Back-country routes are tough because they're not cleared or prepared. It's up to you to avoid snowdrifts!

Hiking with skis

A great way of exploring the wilderness is cross-country skiing. Many trails run for miles over unspoiled terrain. You'll need special skis and boots for this type of skiing.

Cross-country boots fit neatly onto long, narrow skis.

Special gear

Cross-country skis have grooves underneath to grip snow, and can be covered in an extra layer called a **skin** to make uphill treks easier. Light, small boots clip into the skis at the toe. This lets you lift your heels and push forward with plenty of power. Use ski poles to help you move along.

Cross-country skiing lets you explore snowy places more easily than on foot.

EXTREME BUT TRUE The Canadian Ski Marathon is held every year on the world's longest cross-country trail in Quebec, Canada. Skiers choose how many sections of the 99.4 mile (160 km) course they want to cover. Those who ski the whole way (and camp overnight) receive an award.

STAY SAFE

The thrill of speeding down a mountain slope can turn to disaster if you don't use your head and stay safe. Here are some of the main hazards.

Avalanches are huge, fast-moving masses of sliding snow that can bury you completely.

EXTREME BUT TRUE Being exposed to extreme cold for a long time can lead to **hypothermia**, a serious condition that can kill you.

It's a good idea to carry a first aid kit to treat minor injuries such as cuts and scrapes.

Watch out!

If you go too fast you may lose control, especially when turning, so keep steady, and don't attempt slopes that are too hard. Be aware of other people or obstacles ahead, so you don't swerve at the last minute to avoid them.

Keep calm

Bad weather can mean trouble if you're in the back-country or on a remote trail. Heavy snow and thick cloud cause white-outs, where you can't see a thing. Don't panic. Stay calm, find shelter if possible, and wait for the sky to clear. Don't stumble on—you could get hurt or lost.

COOL COMPETITIONS

There are many exciting snow sport races and competitions around the world, including the Winter Olympic Games every four years.

They're fun to watch— or maybe even take part in one day!

A slalom skier skids around a gate. The fastest person with the fewest errors over two events wins.

Slalom racing

Slaloms are downhill races on courses dotted with poles called gates. Skiers weave between the gates as fast as possible, making sure they don't pass any on the wrong side. These fast, dangerous races lead to spectacular crashes!

THRILL SEEKER
Heath Calhoun (U.S.)

FEAT
Competed in **Winter Paralympic Games** after having both legs amputated

WHERE AND WHEN
Vancouver, 2010

Giant jumps

Ski jumpers slide down huge ramps on very large skis, then soar into the air and glide as far as they can. Judges award points for distance but also the quality of the glide and landing.

Board games

Snowboarding events include downhill races, slaloms, jumps, and **halfpipes** held in U-shaped arenas. In **boardercross** races, four to six snowboarders hurtle over bumps and snow banks, each trying to finish first.

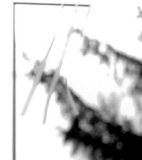

A snowboarder shoots down the steep slope of a halfpipe ramp.

Ski jumpers get points for holding their skis steady and keeping their body straight.

EXTREME BUT TRUE The world record for the longest ski jump is 808.73 feet (246.5m). It was set in 2011 by Norwegian skier Johan Remen Evensen.

GLOSSARY

artificial ski slope
A slope covered with a dense mat of material that acts like snow to help skiers and snowboarders practice downhill runs, turns, and jumps. It is also known as a dry ski slope.

artificial ski slope

back-country
Away from marked ski trails. You need lots of experience before you try back-country skiing.

boardercross
A very difficult snowboarding race that includes jumps and turns, as well as steep and flat sections. You can watch boardercross races in the Winter Olympics.

bunny hill
A very gentle slope used by ski instructors to teach complete beginners the basics of skiing or snowboarding.

halfpipe
A competition held in an arena with sloped sides. Halfpipes were originally made from half sections of huge pipes.

hamstring
One of the stretchy cords (called tendons) that attach muscle to bone behind your knee.

hypothermia
A very dangerous condition in which a person becomes so cold that their body stops working properly. Without medical help, they may die.

lunge
To push forward in one quick, strong movement.

oxygen
An invisible gas in the air around us. We need oxygen to breathe.

parallel

Side by side. Parallel skis are the same distance apart all the way along their length.

parallel skis

skin

A strip of material that sticks to the bottom of a ski and allows it to slide forward but also to grip the snow when pushed backward. Skins help cross-country skiers go uphill.

snowcat

A truck with two sets of tracks to flatten snow on ski runs.

Winter Paralympic Games

A multisport event organized with the Winter Olympic Games. Top athletes with a wide range of disabilities compete in sports including downhill and slalom skiing, snowboarding, and ice sledge hockey.

snowcat

WEBSITES

www.ussa.org/global/getting-started
Find all the information you need to start skiing or boarding, including clubs near you.

www.fis-ski.com
Read about top skiing and snowboarding events from the International Ski Federation.

www.abc-of-snowboarding.com/snowboarding-tricks
Learn how to do great snowboarding tricks and stunts.

INDEX